# UNDERGROUND

## SHANE W. EVANS

SQUARE
FISH

A NEAL PORTER BOOK
ROARING BROOK PRESS
NEW YORK

*Thank you, God, for sharing this vision with me
and allowing me to hold the gift to illuminate it.
This book is dedicated to Pastor Alice. She has shown me what it means to give,
and through the light in her spirit she has transformed a community and helped
so many to freedom. God bless you, mama . . . God bless you.*

Imprints of Macmillan
175 Fifth Avenue, New York, NY 10010
mackids.com

Roaring Brook Press is a division of Holtzbrinck Publishing Holdings Limited Partnership.
Square Fish and the Square Fish logo are trademarks of Macmillan and
are used by Roaring Brook Press under license from Macmillan.

Macmillan books may be purchased for business or promotional use.
For information on bulk purchases, please contact the Macmillan Corporate and Premium
Sales Department at (800) 221-7945 x5442 or by e-mail at specialmarkets@macmillan.com.

Library of Congress Cataloging-in-Publication Data
Evans, Shane.
Underground / Shane W. Evans.
p.      cm.
"A Neal Porter book."
1. Underground Railroad—Juvenile literature.  2. Fugitive slaves—United States—History—
19th century—Juvenile literature.  3. Antislavery movements—United States—History—
19th century—Juvenile literature.  4. Abolitionists—United States—History—
19th century—Juvenile literature.  I. Title.
E450.E94 2010          973.7′115—dc22          2010007735

ISBN 978-1-59643-538-4  (Roaring Brook hardcover)
5  7  9  10  8  6

ISBN 978-1-250-05675-7  (Square Fish paperback)
1  3  5  7  9  10  8  6  4  2

Originally published in the United States by Neal Porter Books/Roaring Brook Press
First Square Fish Edition: 2015
Book designed by Jennifer Browne
Square Fish logo designed by Filomena Tuosto

LEXILE: BR

The darkness.

The escape.

We are quiet.

We run.

We crawl.

We rest.

We make
new friends.

Others help.

Some don't make it.

We are tired.

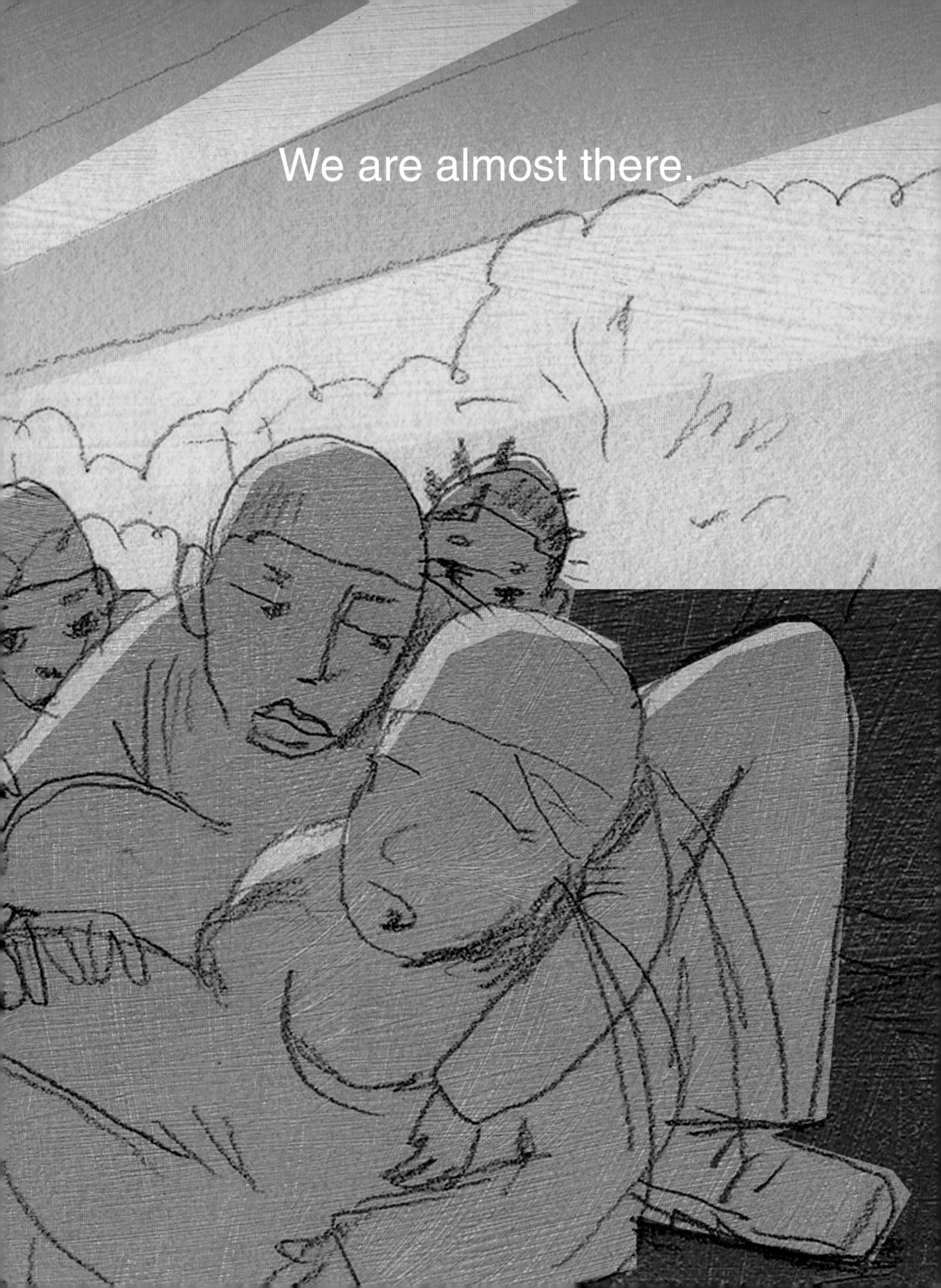
We are almost there.

The light.

The Sun.

Freedom.

I am free.
He is free. She is free.
We are free.

From the early 1600s, before there even was a United States of America until the abolition of slavery in 1865, people could lawfully own a fellow human being. This means that they could buy, sell, and even auction off other humans as if they were livestock. Today it is hard to imagine what it would be like to be "owned" by another person, but less than 150 years ago it was a common practice.

Freedom is a word that means so many different things to so many different people. But for slaves it meant the right to wake up and live as they pleased, something most of us take for granted.

Throughout the course of slavery, there were always people who ran toward freedom. Early in the 1800s, a group of bold men and women formed the Underground Railroad, determined to free themselves and others. Like most children, when I first learned about it I imagined an underground train carrying people off to freedom. Then I learned that it was actually a complex network of everyday people who helped, at their own peril, shine a light on an estimated thirty thousand slaves' paths to freedom by giving them shelter, food, and directions for the long, hard journey.

Look in your own neighborhood and find where the spirit of the underground remains. It is still all around us as we strive for freedom every day.

I dedicate this book to Pastor Alice, who runs an organization called True Light Resources Center. She helps free people today by finding food and shelter for the homeless and women and children in need. Someday she will be mentioned among our greatest heroes—Harriet Tubman, Sojourner Truth, and Fredrick Douglass—who all helped others reach freedom in their own way. I am proud to call her my neighbor.

*Shane W. Evans*

To see a video interview with the author/illustrator
and to learn more about this book go to:
www.shaneevans.com/underground

*A portion of the proceeds from this book will go to
the True Light Resource Center, a true light in a community.*